Conversation Skills Secrets

How You Can Extend Your Influence In Conversations To Have More Success In Life

By

Joshua Larson

Table of Contents

Introduction

Poor conversation skills alienate you from other people. They create awkward situations, and prevent close relationships from forming. If you suffer from a lack of conversation skills, you know the pain of trying to make friends and get people to take you seriously all too well.

This book is your solution to revolutionizing your conversation skills. You will learn how to hold a great conversation and how to relate to people more solidly. You will also learn some of the top conversation mistakes to avoid. From making conversations more meaningful to avoiding awkward silences, everything you need to know about conversation skills can be found in these pages. By the end of this book, you will be a pro at starting and maintaining fascinating and deep conversations with others.

You may wonder what this book offers that the millions of other books on conversation skills don't. The simple answer is: Science. I have embarked on a scientific research mission to discover what makes a great conversation and what makes a bad one. The results of my studies are presented here, to help you.

Imagine being able to talk to anyone without shyness. Imagine turning your conversations from basic small talk into meaningful, deep connections – solid friendships or good business connections. This is all possible using the science-backed tips included in these pages.

Before I embarked on this research mission, I was a terrible conversationalist. I used to hem and haw and drive people away. Awkward small talk aggravated me, and I just couldn't figure out how to get past that and start talking about more touching subjects. But with the research I performed, I was able to break past that habit and have actual fun conversations with complete strangers. My social life drastically improved almost overnight. It took effort on my part, but my new approach to having conversations paid off well in the end.

If you want to enjoy the same success, then read this book. These are the same tips that worked for me. Once you try them, I promise that they will work for you too. Improve your conversation skills, your business networking, your social life, and your ability to connect to random strangers. Grow your network beyond the familiar and get yourself out there. Become known as the best conversationalist around.

Conversation skills may seem inaccessible and alien at the moment, but they are skills that you can learn and polish with time. If you start practicing today with the skills you learn in this book, you will become a great conversationalist in no time.

Practice makes perfect, so with some more work, you will be a great conversationalist rather quickly.

But why stall any longer? Don't wait to start improving your conversation skills. Don't endure another day of banal, boring small talk and missed connections. Jump right in and start finding out how to develop better conversation skills today. Start reading this book and notice the changes that happen practically overnight in your life.

Chapter 1: Fundamental Techniques in Handling People

Conversation skills are the means by which you connect to others, transmit information, and form an impression of yourself. What you don't realize is that these skills give you a massive amount of control over your relationship with the other person. You can seize that control by learning how to handle people properly through conversation, transforming simple verbal exchanges into the scenarios and relationships that you want. Here are some of the fundamental techniques by which you can gain and exercise that spectacular control.

Don't Criticize, Condemn, or Complain

How negative are you in conversation? I bet you don't even realize how much negativity you put off when you speak, thus accidentally repelling people before they even have a chance to become good connections. While you think you are just being relatable, you are actually being negative and creating your own hurdles to great conversation.

Let's consider first how you might start a conversation. A lot of people think that commiserating is a great conversation starter. You might say, "Nasty weather, huh?" or "Today is dragging, isn't it?" What people fail to realize when they say things like this is that they are complaining and starting a conversation with negativity. The other person might respond with a laugh or agreement, but the conversation pretty much grinds to a screeching halt right there. The reason is because no one wants to entertain a conversation that consists entirely of complaining.

In another common case, what if someone tells you that they love a certain artist? If you respond by criticizing that artist, you are inadvertently criticizing the other person for his or her taste. That right there is inherent negativity that can end the conversation abruptly and sour the other person's impression of you. Criticizing anything about the other person – their clothes, their mannerisms, how they do their job – will kill the conversation rapidly and breed resentment rather than fostering friendship.

And finally, if a person tells you that he is part of a religion or does something you disagree with and you promptly condemn it, you are creating separation rather than relation. This severs any potential bond, causing a friendship to stop forming immediately. You may think you are just stating an opinion, but you are really creating a wall of negativity that the other person feels unable and unwilling to breach.

The simple key here is to avoid using tons of negativity when first meeting a person. Don't sprinkle complaints, criticisms, or condemnations in your speech. Use more positivity for more positive results.

A study by the John Templeton Foundation illustrates this fundamental key in handling others.[1] Positivity is appreciated far more than negativity. Happy brains reject negativity and negative people in favor of more positive, upbeat views. Being positive will make you radiate warmth, which will attract people to you. The sad thing is, most people don't know this and this is why most conversations are lifeless before you even know what happened.

This hardly means that you need to fake it and pretend to like everything about another person. But you should find points of common interest to bond over. For instance, if the other person loves fly fishing, you don't have to lie and say, "Oh, fly fishing is my favorite!" Instead, try to find a point of common interest by saying, "I'm not a big fly fisherman, but I do love the outdoors. I once went on a deep sea fishing expedition outside of Cuba. What's your favorite thing about fishing?"

Or if you don't care for someone's taste, outfit, or something else, don't criticize the person. Instead, try to find one nice thing about him or her that you can sincerely compliment. People can sense insincerity, so don't lie. You must be genuine when you make compliments. If you can't find anything to compliment, then just keep your mouth shut or change the subject. This applies to the grade school saying, "If you have nothing nice to say, don't say anything at all!"

When it comes to condemning, it's best to keep judgement to yourself. No one really wants to hear your negative opinions. You will get people to like you and want to be around you a lot more if you don't offer judgement over everything.

Negativity Is Contagious

Believe it or not, negativity is contagious. This is why people may form a sort of bond over negativity, but that bond is not healthy or conducive to anything great. This is also people may not like to be around you because your negative vibes make them feel more negative.

A study published in the journal of Consumer Research exposed some consumers to negative opinions of a product and others to positive opinions.[2] Then these consumers were asked to sample the product and write their own reviews. Those who were originally exposed to a positive opinion generally wrote positive reviews, and vice versa. This shows that one person's negative opinions can rub off on another, creating a cycle of negativity that keeps spreading.

Thus, it follows that negativity is not necessarily a good thing. You start a conversation negatively and you only spread negative vibes. Positivity spreads, too, and it feels much better. You can make more people like you and respond to you positively by being positive yourself.

Give Honest and Sincere Appreciation

People are beings of ego. The one thing that makes them happy – and thus more receptive to you – is feeling appreciated. Since sincerity can be sensed by others, you should give sincere and honest compliments or thanks to get others to warm up to you.

Though we already touched on this in the previous section, let's explore it with a bit more depth. When you want someone to like you, do what you want, adopt your view on something, or otherwise do what you want, you must trigger a release of dopamine and serotonin within their brains to make them happy. They begin to associate you with happiness and thus they are more eager to please you.

One of the easiest and most efficient means of accomplishing this is to compliment someone and appeal to their ego. Compliments activate a person's striatum, which is the same region of the brain activated by cash or the promise of other rewards.[3] In other words, compliments act as motivators, and will encourage a person to pursue a conversation because they see the compliment as a reward for talking to you.

A compliment is essentially a "mini-high" because of this striatum activation and the ensuing rush of feel-good neurochemicals, like dopamine.[3] People want to get more of that high so they keep pursuing the conversation. The end result is a person who hangs on your every word. Use this to your advantage by complimenting people and seeing how it can lead to conversations and lasting bonds.

One interesting way to do this is to show interest in what a person has to say. Don't just talk to them, waiting for your turn to speak. Actually listen to what they have to say. Then ask thoughtful questions that demand more than a yes or no answer. People love to talk about themselves and feel as if they are being listened to, so listening will certainly spark a conversation that lasts.[4]

Another way is to provide a compliment as an icebreaker. Say someone is wearing a pretty dress. You know that person chose that dress with the intent of arousing admiration in others. Stimulate that person's ego with a compliment on how the dress flatters her and how the color is just beautiful. You are essentially doing exactly what that person wants, and thus you make her night.

Furthermore, appearance or physical compliments are always ego-boosting, but complimenting a person's kind nature, excellent progress at work, or recent accomplishments is even more profound. You will make more of an impact on the person's mood and inspire a deeper conversation. Say someone you want to get to know just won an award and is carrying it around, beaming. Ask him or her about the award and provide ample congratulations.

More interesting and unique compliments tend to stroke egos more efficiently. You could say "Nice dress," and get a simple "Thank you." Conversation over. Or you could take it a step further and spark more lasting conversation by asking about the story behind the dress. If you say something interesting that makes the other person give more than a yes or no answer, then you are on the route to a successful and lasting conversation.

Different Types of Listening

As you already know now, listening strokes another person's ego. But there are different types of listening. Learning the best form of listening and how to exhibit your attention and absorption is one of the fundamentals to handling other people in conversation.[4]

The first type of listening is hearing, or discriminative listening. Something comes into your ears but you don't necessarily interact with the information or respond to it. You can hear traffic din, for instance. Hearing is the least effective type of listening.

Then you have comprehension listening. This is where you actually bother to pick out sounds and try to make sense of them. You might practice this when a friend is shouting at you across the noisy bar or you are trying to hear an important broadcast on the radio over static.

Next comes critical listening. This is where you evaluate what you are hearing and make inferences or judgements about it. Usually this type of listening is the kind people employ when they are listening to you while impatiently awaiting their chance to talk and spout their newly formed opinion. Critical listening can turn into biased listening, where you skew what you are taking in to fit what you want to hear.

In appreciative listening, we are trying to learn by listening. This is how you listen to your professor or boss. While this type of listening is flattering because it shows your unbiased attention, it is not great for personal relationships because it is entirely formal and also selfish. You are only listening to learn or get information for yourself.

Take appreciative listening a step further by using sympathetic listening. This is when you learn from a person's talking in order to come up with the best reply. You use this listening when your friend is sobbing about a break-up, for instance. It is great for when people are complaining or need a shoulder to cry on, but it is not so great when you are first meeting a person.

Empathetic listening or dialogic listening are the two types that are most flattering and more conducive to good conversation, particularly with people you don't know extremely well. Empathetic is where you attempt to identify with the person, thus creating points of relation and identification. Dialogic is where you seek elements in what someone says to which you can reply to form a deeper bond. Dialogic is the path to conversation because you are both exchanging information to get to know each other and lay a foundation for future discussions.

Eventually, once you cross the threshold of being acquaintances and actually get to know each other, you can employ relationship listening. This is where you absorb what a person says and apply elements from your past shared history to formulate the best replies. Conversations are usually loaded with emotion and history, and you can freely talk about yourself as well as the other person.

Relationship listening is the type of close listening you should use when you know someone well. It is expected of you when you enter a relationship of any kind with another person. Avoiding this type of listening when you get to know a person can lead to coldness or distance in the relationship and a lack of profundity.

Arouse in the Other Person an Eager Want

Why will people talk to you? Why will they bother to get to know you and have contact with you again? Because they want to. To start a good conversation that endures, and a subsequent relationship, you must arouse an eager want in the other participant. If you fail to do this, the other person will lose interest and walk away, seeking another conversation that actually does captivate their attention.

Combine the Previous Two Principles

To get a conversation going, you must inspire an eager want for the conversation in the other person so that they desire more contact and further verbal exchange. While this may sound challenging, it is relatively simple, drawing on the previous two principles visited in this chapter. All you have to do is radiate positivity and give someone sincere appreciation. These two things will arouse a desire for more connection within the other person without fail.

Use Ethos to Your Advantage

Another way to inspire want in people is to evoke their emotions. A banal conversation about the weather is not going to inspire emotion. Thus, it won't form a major impact on the other person's brain. The conversation becomes easily forgettable. But if you talk about things that inspire emotion, you stick out in a person's brain and open up a deep well of topics to converse about.

Emotional appeals tend to make people support you more.[5] So to get someone to like you, you want to use emotional appeal. Emotional appeal is also a very effective in persuasion and advertising, which I cover in more depth a little later.

The reason emotion appeal works is because the brain tends to remember how someone makes you feel far more than what the person says or does.[5] You remember emotions quite vividly. For instance, you probably remember the humiliation your high school bully inflicted upon you far more vividly than anything else about that bully.

It may not behoove you to discuss dead puppies to make someone cry in a first conversation. But bringing up things that people are passionate about or feel strongly about is an effective means to start a conversation that may turn into more. Passion is one of the strongest and most appropriate emotions that is appealing when you converse with someone you are not particularly close to.

Observe a person and glean some clues about what he or she might be passionate about. Most people make it obvious. A person who refuses the meat entrée might just be vegetarian, so you can ask about his or her views on animal cruelty or health. A person with a "Say No To Straws" emblem on his gym bag is probably passionate about the environment. Or you could just simply ask a person about his or her passions and then base a conversation on that.

Mirroring and Points of Common Interest: The Importance of Similarities

Finding points that you can relate on is the next big step in handling people. You want to form a bond. People tend to like those who are similar to them[6], so finding similarities and common interests is essential to creating any sort of bond beyond a passing exchange of pleasantries.

Rumor has it that opposites attract, but an influential study proves that that couldn't be further from the truth. When forming relationships, people seek like-minded individuals.[6] People will determine if they like you based on how closely you follow their beliefs or indulge in their pleasures of choice. It is also shown that sought-out similarities go much deeper than a shared love of golf or some other mundane hobby: They become much more important when it comes to politics, religion, or other issues that people hold dear. You may be able to set your differences aside to enjoy hobbies or work together, but your best friends will usually share your views on issues that you hold close to your heart.[6]

The easiest way to form a bond is to find things you have in common and talk about that. That is Conversation Etiquette 101 that you can read in literally any article or book about conversation skills. You probably already know this fact quite well.

But I will share two things that you probably didn't know. The first is that you probably drive away bonds without even realizing it. This is because you work on creating differences or divides when conversing with people, instead of attempting to find commonalities. For instance, when a person talks about being a dog person, you immediately scrap that bonding opportunity by stating that you're a cat person. It would be far better to simply say, "I'm an animal lover, too." You don't need to love dogs, you just need to share your similar adoration for animals to appeal to the other person's hard-wired desire for a like-minded conversation partner.

When a person mentions an interest, try to find something you enjoy that is similar to that, instead of simply stating that you don't share that interest. This makes you a more relatable and magnetic conversationalist. It allows for bonds based on similarities even when you don't match each other perfectly in the interest department.

When it comes to deeply personal things, like religion and politics, you are wise to steer clear of those topics until you actually decide that you like each other enough to talk more. Not only are these topics extremely sensitive and divisive, but they are quite rude in conventional conversation. Save that for the second conversation if you can.

The other bit I'm going to share with you is a sneaky little trick known as mirroring. The actual hard science behind the success of mirroring is a bit paltry. There are remarkably few studies supporting it. But there is an abundance of anecdotal evidence supporting it, so it is at least worth a try.

Mirroring is mentioned frequently in neurolinguistic programming, a controversial pseudoscience involving the use of words and body language to program your own mind or the minds of others. Again, NLP is primarily supported anecdotally. But the success rates people claim to have it with are eerily great, suggesting that there may be something to it.

In mirroring, you mimic the other person. You wait a few seconds after the person makes a face or pulls away and then you do the same thing subtly. Doing this makes you appear drastically similar to the other person, inspiring a close bond and a sense of companionship basically out of thin air. The other person has no idea what you are doing – he or she just knows that he or she likes you a lot suddenly.

Get Personal More Quickly

A study[7] proves that two people who converse about more personal and deeply emotional topics are more likely to become best friends. Keeping things purely non-personal is a good way to keep a conversation both cold and uninteresting. The more personal you get, the more of a bond you form and the more of a want you inspire in the other person.

In the study, strangers were broken into pairs and asked to rate how much they liked each other privately. Once this feedback was obtained, the pairs were asked to ask each other 36 deeply personal questions, in three sets that become increasingly probing. At the end, they were asked to stare into each other's eyes for up to four minutes without looking away. After this activity, they were asked to rate how much they liked each other again. Compared to a control group who talked about the weather and other banalities, the group who asked the personal questions liked each other much more at the conclusion of the study. It appeared these deeply personal questions broke the ice and bonded them more than small talk bonded the control group.[7]

Getting personal does not mean that you need to get embroiled in a conversation about politics or inquire about a person's private marital relations. But it means going beyond the mundane and asking some very interesting, thought-provoking questions that a person has probably never been asked before. You will certainly make a lasting impression and form a tighter bond.

Here are several of the questions used in the study:

1. If a crystal ball could you tell your future, would you want to know?
2. When was the last time you sang to someone? What was the song?
3. What are you most grateful for in your life?
4. If you could change one thing about your life, what would it be?
5. What would be your definition of a perfect day?
6. What do you value most in friendship?
7. What is your most treasured memory?
8. When was the last time you cried?
9. What was your most embarrassing moment?

As you can see, these questions are very personal. Yet they bonded people. They are also unique and emotional.

Chapter 2: Ways to Make Other People Like You

It feels good to be liked. But being liked also comes with benefits. People who like you will do more favors for you, and will give you more ego-boosting compliments to build your confidence, which only makes you more attractive to others. Friends bring with them new connections and new opportunities in life, business, leisure, you name it. And, above all, being popular makes other people assume that you are all right, so they like you too. The more friends you have, the more friends you make, according to Dr. Robert Cialdini's Social Proof Principle.[8] Everyone wants to do what everyone else is doing, so if you're popular, you encourage others to like you just by being you.

But being liked is not just a natural talent that some people are born with. Yes, some people are born with the inherent skills of charisma. These skills are possible for anyone to learn, however. If you are not a naturally charismatic and radiant person, if you were never the popular kid in high school, and if you have trouble making friends, there is still plenty of hope for you.

Getting people to like you is as simple as appealing to human psychology. Through various scientific methods, you can make yourself more attractive to others and thus earn more friends and valuable connections. You just have to learn the tricks of the trade. Once you learn them, you will enjoy a vastly improved social life and many more social connections.

Cialdini's Principle of Social Proof

In the next chapter, you will learn much more about Dr. Robert Cialdini's groundbreaking work on influence and persuasion. But now you will learn about one principle that is sure to get people to like you: his principle of social proof.

According to this principle, if you appear to be a hot commodity, more people will want you. This works when picking up people at the bar or networking at a swanky event or just trying to make friends. If you show that someone likes you, then others think, "He must not be so bad. I can like him too."[8]

If you show up to an event or party alone, you must rely on conversation skills to get others to like you. It can be hard to break the ice that way, particularly when everyone is sealed up in their own cliques and busy chatting with their own friends. It can also be tough if you are shy. It is far more helpful to show up with a buddy to prove that you are likable.

In the event that you have to be alone, try to find other loners and bond with them. Once you have collected a little group of people to talk to, you appear more likable. Then others will gravitate toward you.

Another one of Cialdini's principles also applies to being well-liked. If you appear to be in short supply, the demand will increase for you. People operate on a scarcity mentality, where they have to have something that will soon run out. Appearing busy or unable to stay for long can make people feel more inclined to engage you in conversation.[8]

Smile

Smiles are universal expressions of warmth, gratitude, and affection. All cultures engage in smiling. This is why smiling is so important, because it communicates a lot without words.

When you smile, you appear warm and non-threatening and thus you encourage others to approach you. And you appear like you are a confident, positive person who is not afraid to smile, even when things are going wrong. Being the first to smile at someone is the same as being the first to approach them. In fact, a smile can be considered a type of approach, or icebreaker.

A certain region of the brain called the orbitofrontal *cortex* activates when people see a smile. This area of the brain is responsible for seeing sensory rewards, or pretty things. It is the part of the brain that goes, "Ooh, shiny!" A smile causes this part of the brain to light up on fMRIs, suggesting that people equate smiles with sensory rewards. So when you smile at someone, you are lighting up his or her brain.[9]

This study also suggests that people find smiling faces more attractive since their brains have the same reaction to smiling as they do to seeing beautiful faces.[9] Even if you are not a supermodel, a smile can make you that much more lovely. People are more receptive to attractive faces. You will get liked more if you appear more attractive to others.

Smiling also causes some interesting chemistry to happen inside your own body. A smile will release neuropeptides, which fight stress, and dopamine, serotonin, and norepinephrine. Thus, smiling helps you relax and restore your good mood. This can also make you more likable and approachable, because you are feeling good yourself. Just like how negativity is contagious, positivity is too.[1]

One study shows that 60% of people can tell whether a smile is genuine or fake.[10] That rate shoots up to 66% in a party atmosphere.[10] Genuine smiles tend to get better reactions out of people than fake ones. So even if you don't feel like smiling much, think of something like cute puppies or your crush, and smile like you mean it. This will make people like you so much more.[9]

Show Genuine Interest in Other People

Again, since people can smell fakeness from a mile away, being fake in conversation is seldom wise.[10]

People tend to be poor judges of lies, but they can tell something isn't right. So faking interest in a person is only going to lead to more awkward and uninteresting conversation.

Instead, show genuine interest. Ask people questions and try to learn more about them. Should a person bring up something you know nothing about, profess your ignorance and request for them to educate you. This keeps conversations going.

Should a person really bore you, don't just feign interest. Shift the conversation onto more interesting grounds by asking a question or making a relevant comment. Keep things entertaining for everyone. That is one extremely valuable skill in a good conversationalist.

The reason genuine interest is so important is because people love to feel important. If you show interest, then you give someone that sense of importance that releases all sorts of feel-good hormones in their brains.

Remember a Person's Name

What happens when you say someone's name? Certain centers of the brain activate in interesting ways. The medial frontal cortex gets particularly active.[11] This indicates that when you hear your own name, versus the names of others, you get excited and take special notice. From experience, you know this to be true.

Hearing one's own name is an example of self-representational behavior.[11] It triggers the medial frontal cortex because this is the part of the brain where sense of self and personality is formed.[11] When you see your reflection in a mirror and recognize yourself, your reaction is much different than when you see someone else in the mirror beside you. The reason for this is because a different part of your brain activates when you see or hear anything pertaining to yourself.

This is why teachers find it useful to memorize their students' names on the first day of class. Teachers who do this have better bonds with their students and work better with the classroom as a whole because they make students feel good through self-representational models. They can lose that bond if they unintentionally forget or mess up a student's name.

Therefore, remembering a person's name is not just good manners. It is a scientific means by which you can get someone to like you. You make people happy and prove that you think them important when you bother to remember their names. Get their medial frontal cortexes happy by using their real names!

Encourage Others to Talk about Themselves and Listen Well

Again, when a person talks about him- or herself, try to listen very well. People love to talk about themselves, so encourage this. The resulting dopamine flood will make them associate you with feeling good and thus they will like you more.

Furthermore, you can encourage people by asking them questions about themselves. These questions shouldn't be run of the mill "yes or no" questions. Actually asked involved questions, like: "How does that work?" or "How do you do that?" or "How does that make you feel?"

Speak to Others' Interests

Speaking to a person's interests keeps their attention held. No one likes to talk about something that is disinteresting to them. So you want to find topics that you both can enjoy discussing. Finding out what a person is into is helpful, but you should also find out what a person doesn't want to talk about.

People don't like to be rude (usually), so no one will tell you outright when they are bored or offended. But the signs are clear. You just need to pay attention. People can communicate a lot non-verbally, through facial expressions, body language, and subconscious signals. A person will start looking around the room, eyeing the exit, fidgeting, or even giving fake smiles when he or she is anxious to leave a conversation that is no longer satisfying.[10] When you spot these signs, it is a good cue to change the subject.

You may need to try many different subjects to find something to talk about, particularly with a shy or reticent person who lacks good conversation skills himself. Switching between topics can be jarring, but just keep trying until you find something that you can both relate on.

Current events are always effective conversation starters. Most people are interested in current events. If that doesn't work, ask the other person what his or her interests are and build a conversation on that. Of course, always seek commonalities that you can both bond over. Think of other things most people enjoy: commenting on what is going on during the networking event/party where you are meeting, food, other people, hobbies, work, accomplishments. These are all decent topics that can kick off a conversation.

Make People Feel Important

Flattering someone in a genuine way is always a good way to score brownie points and get someone to like you. Paying attention is one way to make someone feel important, but there are other ways as well.

Maslow's Hierarchy of Needs is a social theory that points to how people need and want to feel. A person who is secure, happy, and satisfied is typically socially satisfied.[12] Most people are insecure, however, and benefit from hearing that they are socially liked and needed. You want to appeal to that need for social satisfaction by letting someone know that he is important to others and serves a vital function in society.

Maslow's hierarchy of needs is commonly represented as a pyramid. At the very bottom layer are physical needs implicit to survival – food, shelter, water, sex. The next level up is the need for safety and security. People tend to worry most about these things when they are jeopardized, such as in a war-torn and poverty-stricken third world country. In first world countries like ours, most people have these intrinsic needs met, so they are free to worry about the upper levels of the pyramid.

The third level of the pyramid is love. People need to feel loved, at least by someone. Then there is esteem, where a person needs to feel good about himself and his accomplishments and needs confidence to approach life. At the very pinnacle of the pyramid is the need for self-actualization, which basically details the sense of accomplishing your purpose in life and somehow furthering the world with your personal contributions, while using your abilities at their greatest capacity and unlocking all of your potential.

When you let a person know how important he is, you satisfy the three upper levels of the pyramid, or his need to be loved, to have esteem, and to fulfill his potential in life by actually mattering. You also let him know that his life's work is recognized and not wasted. Telling someone his accomplishments are important is the highest form of flattery. That's a big deal according to Abraham Maslow.

Basically, congratulate someone on his work, or ask what he does for a living and then comment about how important that job is. If a person is well-known, or at least known by you, be sure to say that so that you appear like a big fan.

Wear Red

This weird little tip is indeed out there, but it works. The human brain is wired to respond well to red. Wearing red, even just in your hat or tie, can make others like you a lot more.[13] It makes others assume you are a warm, trustworthy, and relatable person.

In a study, men approached women wearing red lipstick the most often.[13] People wearing red were also ranked "more attractive." And women tend to view men wearing red or with red hair as more approachable and more suitable for romantic pursuits.[13] The conclusion is that while red can be the color of pain and danger, it is also somehow an attractive, warm, and even seductive color. People seem drawn to red. They will certainly notice you if you wear it.

Try red lipstick or a red dress as a woman, or a red tie or shirt as a man. Red hair color can also make you more attractive. Consider a red coat or hat in winter months, and a red umbrella on rainy days. In little ways, up the amount of red you wear to become more likable.

Chapter 3: How to Win People Over to Your Way of Thinking

The art of persuasion is one that many people have dedicated their entire lives to researching. Of course everyone wants to be successfully persuasive. Imagine the power you would have over others if you could change their thinking to match yours with just a few smooth words. Based on politicians and other influential or manipulative people, it is more than possible to gain this kind of power, but how to do it is often elusive to those who don't naturally possess this skill.

Persuasion is something some people are born with – but it is hardly elusive if you know what it actually entails. Science shows us some convenient and easy ways to basically change others' minds and persuade people to your way of thinking quite effortlessly. And it doesn't even involve high levels of psychological warfare, hypnosis, or even manipulation. In fact, the best way to be persuasive is to use the previous principles, and some new ways you are about to learn, to become likable to others. This sways people to your point of view without much effort on your part, and it's easier than you think.

Six Principles of Influence

Dr. Robert Cialdini is an expert in influence and how to persuade other people to your way of thinking. Studying his work is still popular today because his theories are still accurate. His most prominent work involves six principles of influence, rules that Dr. Cialdini proposed which are still very much applicable today to persuasion.[8]

The first principle is the Principle of Reciprocity. The premise of this principle is "You scratch my back, I scratch yours." If you do someone a favor, he is more likely to do something for you to please you or "pay you back." So if you get someone to come around to your way of thinking, it is because you influence him by making him feel as if he owes you. Doing people little favors is a good way to reap reciprocity.

The next is commitment/consistency. People like things to be consistent with their values. A woman who believes in protecting the environment can be more easily persuaded to donate to a cause that appears to line up with her environmental sentimentality. A couple who is deeply religious will be more likely to agree with church-backed statements. And so on. Find someone's values and figure out how you can align your statements with them.

Social proof is the third principle. This is where people act on the herd mentality and influence each other. It is why trends sweep the nation, videos go viral, and your co-workers will stay later if everyone else does. No one wants to be the odd one out, so everyone jumps on the same bandwagon. To be persuasive, make your cause or idea out to be very popular and trendy, and more people will be on board with it.

Authority is a very useful principle where you get people to trust you because you are some kind of expert. Celebrity endorsements or doctor approvals are selling tactics often employed by product companies. You can use this yourself and convince people that some expert approved of your product, or you can persuade people that you are an expert yourself. No one will take you seriously unless you can somehow prove you're an authority. By the way, it isn't hard to fake authority. Just talking like you know what you are saying, possibly having a diploma in a related field to your subject matter, providing life stories to support your claims, and showing off awards can convince people to take you seriously.

Liking is where you gain more influence over someone the more he likes you. Use tips from the previous chapter to get people to like you, and from there you can be more influential.

Scarcity is the tactic used when radio announcers yell, "Hurry – this sale won't last long!" People want to gobble something up before it's gone. If they think things are in short supply or rare, they are more likely to try to buy it or do it before it's gone forever. This principle plays into the scarcity mindset as well as human competition. If you want to convince people that your way of thinking is right, try to tell them that they need to believe you and act now because time is running out. Imply urgency in how you speak to scare people into having a scarcity mindset.

Show Respect for Others' Opinions

When you show respect for the opinions of others, you prove that you are the bigger person and you are worthy of being listened to. You will gain more friends and followers if you accept the ideas of others, instead of constantly telling people they are wrong.

This plays into the three upper levels of the Maslow Pyramid.[13] You encourage someone to have love, esteem, and even self-actualization by respecting their opinions. It could be argued that respect is a self-need that all people share.

You may be inadvertently disrespectful. Dismissing someone's words is disrespectful, as is blatantly telling a person he is wrong or overlooking the validity that may exist in his statement. Every person believes his opinion is the right one, and is willing to argue that fact even if there is no factual basis to it, but respect is still possible when there is a difference in opinion. Realize that every other person in the world feels right and correct, despite the fact they are not in your eyes, and treat their words as something valid to be acknowledged.

A good way to show respect is to acknowledge what someone says. A simple, "I hear what you are saying" does wonders for another person's self-esteem. Then point out where he may be right, before suggesting your own fact-based argument. You can even agree to disagree, which is an intrinsically respectful thing to do.

When you stroke a person's self-esteem and satisfy the upper three needs of the Maslow Pyramid for him, you make him feel good.[13] He is more inclined to like you and to accept your opinion, out of a combination of Dr. Cialdini's reciprocity and liking principles.[8] To sway someone to your way of thinking, you really need to play on both of Dr. Cialdini's principles and appeal to the other person's upper needs in order to change his mind.

Admit You're Wrong

Showing tender vulnerability by admitting you're wrong is another way to gain some traction with others when swaying them to your way of thinking. You make yourself more human and relatable in this way, and you also convince people that you have a clear idea of right and wrong. This can convince them to take you more seriously when you are right.

When you admit you are wrong, you activate the reciprocity principle.[8] People are far more likely to also admit they are wrong and to accept your opinions in the future more when you do this. They also gain more respect for you.

Admitting that you are wrong can require swallowing some of your pride. It can be difficult to do. But realize how it will make you look better and get more people on your side.

Be Friendly

To further encourage someone's esteem and love needs, you should always be friendly.[13] The surest way to persuade someone or win a disagreement is to be friendly and likable. No one can dismiss you on grounds of, "He's unkind" if you are friendly. Plus, you sway people to like you, which is grounds for the liking principle to take effect.

Put Yourself in Others' Shoes

Before you start to judge or accuse someone of being wrong, consider things from his standpoint. Empathy is a rare yet critical skill, especially in conversation. Having empathy plays into empathetic listening, which you already know is the best type of listening in a conversation.[4]

When you place yourself in someone's shoes, you are using empathy. Empathy is one of the top social skills because it allows you to understand and connect with others, change your perspective, and react in bonding and emotionally appropriate ways.[14] A very complex interplay of neural pathways within the brain enables empathy, which is why many people probably don't engage in it.[14]

When you are empathetic, you don't just express pity or sympathy for another person, but you relate to him and prove to him that he is understood. You engage in more friendly and compassionate behavior. That validates his feelings and makes him feel less alone, which in turn boosts his mood.

A study proves that empathy declines with medical training.[14] Think of how you feel when a doctor seems callous to your needs or dismisses you when you complain of severe pain. It does not feel good at all. Yet when you are talking to someone or hearing his argument about his point of view, you engage in the same callous behavior by not bothering to understand the background from which his opinion has formed.

Taking the time to view life from someone else's shoes can make you more approachable and relatable. But it also allows you to understand someone else's perspective, so that you can form valid arguments that will actually convince him that you are right. You are able to say "I understand why you think that way, and I would too, but here is what I have to say about that."

Sympathize

Sympathy is another form of self-representational behavior that other people respond well to.[11] When a person expresses sorrow, he wants a shoulder to cry on. He wants someone to tell him that it will all be OK. People seek others' sympathy to feel better about their problems and emotions.

Showing someone sympathy can win him over indefinitely. He feels that he can pour out his soul and that builds a great deal of trust. The trust is the foundation for more closeness, so he comes to like you more and more. In the end, the principle of liking comes into play once again.

Another key here is to never be overbearing or condescending with your sympathy. Condescension is something that people can read quite clearly, and it hurts their egos.[10] Fake sympathy is also something people detect and detest. Try to be genuine and come from a place of compassion as opposed to condescension.

Dramatize Your Ideas

The more dramatic your ideas are, the more they stick out to others. People will be won over if you make your ideas seem exciting and great. Selling yourself further convinces people that you are an authority and that you are someone to listen to and trust.[8]

Dramatizing your ideas is not lying or deception. It is the same thing salesmen do, when they wave their arms around and yell about how this is the deal of the century. Those ads may seem silly, but they get people in the door. You want to do the same thing when you are attempting to sway people or win them over. Making your idea sound zany, interesting, dramatic, and life-altering will make people take heed.

The key here is to capture the attention of others. A boring, mundane sales pitch won't sell your idea at all. People will lose interest quickly and move along. But if you draw attention to your ideas by making them more dramatic than they really are, you generate interest and capture attention.

Dale Carnegie is the first person to put a name to this approach in his influential *How to Make Friends and Influence People.* As an expert in human relations, his advice is quite sound. He proposes dramatizing your ideas in order to get people to pay attention, understand clearly what you are saying, and feel more keen on cooperation.[15] Carnegie encourages you to use pictures instead of words, vivid descriptions, and showmanship to sell your ideas in the best way possible.

Chapter 4: How to Change People without Offending Them

People like to say, "Accept me the way I am." But, sometimes, changing a person is necessary. When people are rude or disrespectful, make mistakes, or otherwise cause problems with their behavior, they need correction. How can you change people in a way that doesn't put them on the defensive and create conflict instead of solutions? The answer is tactful conversation that uses positive reinforcement, constructive criticism, and solutions in place of cruel criticism, yelling, and bullying.

If you use these approaches, you can create smooth interactions that lead to positive change. Not using these approaches will offend others, leading to defensiveness and conflict that doesn't get either party anywhere. When people are offended, they tend to get resentful and do things out of spite, as opposed to cooperating. You can encourage cooperation by using a gentler and more scientific-based approach to your criticism.

These tips are great for the workplace, especially if you are a boss. But they can also be helpful in parenting children, or in working through issues in a marriage or friendship. Anytime you must try to change another person to have a better relationship interaction, whip out these tips.

Begin with Praise and Honest Appreciation

When you are about to try to change someone, you are obviously going to point out mistakes they are making or criticize their behavior thus far. Criticism hurts people and puts them on the defensive. People hate being told that they aren't good enough and they need to change. But there's a way to say things that diminishes the hurt.

To soften the blow, you should create a dopamine rush in the person's brain firsthand. You can do this with some praise to pump up his ego. Let a person know, "You are doing great so far! Just a few things that need improvement…." Or say something like, "I like what you did here, and here, and how you did this. Here are the things I want changed."

Always strive to make a person feel important through appreciation.[13] This ties in with the Maslow Hierarchy of Needs we already covered by making a person feel loved, esteemed, and self-actualized.

Call Attention to Mistakes Indirectly

Wording has a surprisingly huge effect on the brain and its subsequent actions. If you word something just the right way, you change the emotional associations and make it sound better than it really is. One way to change others is to call attention to their shortcomings or mistakes in an indirect way that softens the ego blow significantly.

Criticism resounds much more profoundly within a person's ego than praise, as your brain tends to process negative input in a different region and attach more analysis to it.[16] The human brain is wired to respond more deeply to negative things than positive ones because it attaches more biological significance to mistakes. Back in caveman days, a mistake could mean life or death, which is why your evolution tends to value negative feedback more.[16] But the result is that when you say something negative to a person, it sticks with him a lot longer than praise.

That's why calling attention to a mistake calls for some delicacy if you don't want to create a hurtful and potentially hostile reaction in the recipient of your criticism. In the past, bosses were encouraged to assert their dominance and authority by yelling and criticizing. Now that is not so *en vogue*. It is far better to be indirect and kind about things in the workplace.

A good example is when someone makes a mistake at work. You could humiliate them and make them resent you by berating them in front of the whole office. Or you could instead say, "Take a look at Page 9 on the presentation again please." By saying this, you let a person know that there is a mistake, you give them the chance to fix it, and you avoid unleashing any harsh criticism.

Another thing to do is to use softer wording. Consider the difference between the words "take" and "steal." This huge difference illustrates how two words can have the same meaning, but very different insinuations. Instead of accusing someone of stealing something, ask if he took it, for instance. Or instead of telling a person he screwed up the whole software program in a software engineering firm, tell him he transposed some things in the program or that there is a bug.

Softer wording is intrinsic in the passive voice. This means that you should say something like, "There is a problem" instead of "You did this wrong." The passive voice removes some of the blame and simply proposes there's an issue to be addressed.

Talk about Your Own Mistakes

No one is perfect, including you. Diluting criticism can be accomplished by mentioning that you made a mistake too, or you have made a similar mistake in the past. I'll never forget when I scraped my dad's car on the yellow post by a gas pump in high school and he simply told me, "I remember when I did that when I was seventeen, too." His words made me feel so much better, and you will find that doing the same can make your peers feel better, too.

This ties in with the similarities and commonalities we covered in Chapter 1.[1] People relate when they share things in common. Pointing out that you made a mistake yourself at some point is a thing in common that creates a bond.

Ask Questions instead of Giving Direct Orders

A further instance of softer language is making a request or asking a question in place of barking an order. Direct orders sound authoritative and demanding.

Let the Other Person Save Face

Humiliation is a likely result from criticism or trying to change someone. The humiliation gets stronger and uglier when it happens in front of others.[17] Letting a person save face by proving himself or defending himself is crucial to allow him to bounce back from this humiliation and get over any resentment he may develop toward you.

Humiliation is generally the breakdown of a person's value system.[17] It makes a person feels insignificant and smaller than others. The use of humiliation is very effective as a punishment or as an assertion of dominance, such as in hazing rituals for football teams and fraternities, but in relationships, you want to avoid punishment and dominance and instead use positive reinforcement. People tend to want to please others, so their need to save face and avoid humiliation is high on their priority lists.

Humiliation is on par with rejection in terms of pain.[17] It causes brain activity that is quite similar to that experienced when you break a leg or experience some other form of physical pain.[17] It also triggers a lot of brain activity which can lead to memory neurons being formed, making it a traumatic event that is hard to forget.[17] But having a chance to save face can lessen its impact.

Praise Every Improvement

Even the slightest improvement is progress forward. It is a sign someone is changing as you want. If you acknowledge and praise each and every improvement, no matter how small, then you will certainly encourage that behavior to continue.

Since people want to receive praise, praise acts as a sort of conditioning. They will keep performing the desired behavior in order to earn more praise and feel even better. This is why positive reinforcement is a far more effective motivator than negative.[18]

Use Encouragement and Make Faults Seem Easy to Correct

You can further play into the pinnacle of needs, self-actualization, by showing how some improvement can unlock someone's potential and make them even better.[13] Once they see the potential benefit to changing, they won't be so resistant to the idea. Say, "I love what you've been doing but I think you can do even better. Imagine what you can accomplish if you did this, instead of this."

When you do this, you seem like you are helping, rather than criticizing. You are offering a viable solution rather than simply picking at someone. People respond much better to this approach. Always offer encouragement for how a person can be better, instead of telling them simply what they have done wrong.

You want to also use lots of positive reinforcement as opposed to negative. The result is more positivity in the interaction and fewer hurt feelings. Science shows that positive reinforcement is much more helpful and beneficial than negative reinforcement in a large variety of scenarios.[18] People want to please, especially if they feel like everyone else is doing it, so they are more likely to go after your praise than your criticism. Plus, people will give up if you never offer praise but always have something negative to say.

Chapter 5: Business

When it comes to business, many people are at a loss. Conversation is so key to good business. You want to make meaningful connections, you want to get people to like you, you want to appear professional, you want to attract wealth, you want to be approachable but also serious – it can be confusing and complicated. The three keys to business conversations are understanding power games and dominance, professional expectations, and reading social cues.

How to Deal with an Authority Figure and Have a Conversation when Being on the Low-Power End

In almost every relationship (especially business ones, where a clear hierarchical system is in place), one party has greater power than the other. If you are on the low end of the power spectrum, it can make communication more challenging. You may feel as if you have no power or no voice and nothing you say will be taken seriously.

This eternal power struggle is the root of many problems at work. It results in you being ignored and overlooked, not credited for your ideas, or not invited to participate in brainstorming sessions. It results in no raises and no promotions. And it results in your unhappiness.

If you are lucky, you have a great boss who treats you like an equal and a team member. But not everyone has that. Most bosses enjoy their positions of power and some even abuse their power. Here is how to approach a boss who may lack in empathy or humility and treats you like the low man on the totem pole.

Understanding Dominance

In each organization is some type of hierarchy. Humans and primates are masters of showing dominance without fighting.[19] Your boss is in a position above you. In order to maintain this position, he must assert his authority continually by being dominant over you. Some bosses assert authority by being great team leaders and silently showing their strength rather than their dominance, but many assert authority by demeaning and belittling you, constantly proving their higher status and power.

Power games are hardly anything new. Since the beginning of time, rulers have used manipulation, humiliation, fear, and obscene wealth to show and gain dominance.[19] They expect and demand submission from those underneath them.[19] If you are in such a work environment, then your voice is quieted and your choices are limited by a dominant boss figure or board of directors. You are made to fear for your job and even feel as if what you have to say doesn't matter or isn't good enough.

This hardly means that you can't speak up and have conversations to share your ideas. You just have to learn your place within the hierarchy and act within it in an acceptable way that appeals to your boss. That being said, you should also do what you can to gain some dominance to move up in the company hierarchy. There will be more about this in the next section as well.

Human dominance is hardly a linear model.[19] There are many ups and downs and a constant struggle to maintain the status quo, which is poorly understood by science.[19] A dominant person is under constant threat of losing status, and he knows this, which increases his stress and pressure. This is also why bosses love to play head games and engage in power struggles that seem pointless to everyone else.

The best way to show your submission is to acknowledge a toxic dominant figure's dominance. This act appeals to his ego and makes him like you more. Essentially, be willing to kiss butt if you have to. But show your willingness to take charge, your innovation, and your voice as well to prove that you have what it takes to one day take over his job when he vacates it. It's a delicate balance you must learn to walk: show dominance but be submissive when talking to your authority figures. Some people call this delicate balance respect, others call it playing the game.

Use Body Language

Submissive body language is also crucial when approaching authority figures to speak. A dominant figure will stand there with his head high, shoulders thrown back, spine straight, and chest pushed out.[19] This dominant posture works because it creates the illusion of height, and for some reason human beings look up to those who are taller than they are.[19]

To be submissive, you should appear shorter by relaxing your shoulders, lowering your head, and even curving your spine. Basically, relaxing will give you a more submissive posture.[19] Doing this gives the signal that you are not a threat to contend with, so you don't attract as much cruelty, ridicule, and humiliation in an attempt to keep you down.

Keeping a submissive stance does not mean you have to give up your confidence. Having a confident, dominant stance is important to further your career when working with your equals. But when addressing a boss from your own low-power state, you must work within the confines of your hierarchical system, and being submissive is what is expected of you. You will make a better impression this way when you adopt some submission while talking to your boss. Remember, bad impressions stick around longer and mean more than good ones, so you want to avoid that by all means.[16]

Gain Attention

No matter how hard you work, you won't gain any traction or favor with your boss if you fly under the radar. You must gain your boss's attention. This ties in with dramatizing your ideas and gaining favor with others by being friendly.

Being noticed does involve sticking your neck out and raising your voice a bit. If you are shy, this can take some personal work to accomplish. You won't be noticed if you remain mousy and don't try to attract attention, however.

Speak first and speak fast. In various studies, a deep voice is valued more than a high one, as it's considered more dominant.[20] To make your voice heard, speak deeply. But speak at a volume that people can hear, as well. Women especially struggle with this, but a study has found that even women seeking leadership roles or trying to be taken seriously fare better if they have deep voices. Deep voices are also confused with ugliness, so a low-pitched woman will seem both authoritative and unattractive.[20]

Speaking eloquently is also highly valued. If you use short, succinct sentences that make a great deal of sense, you will be more valued in conversation. No one has the patience for a long-winded diatribe that doesn't touch on any clear points, since humans usually have an attention span of 8 seconds.[21] Once you capture their attention with a great hook, they will likely only be willing to listen for five minutes to possibly twenty in older adults.[21]

You will gain far more favor and have better luck communicating ideas by keeping it short but sweet. Make sure you enunciate clearly, use fairly big words that people are still likely to know, and pronounce things correctly to show that you are intelligent enough to know what you're talking about. Avoid wordiness and repetitiveness that will go over the time limit for someone's attention span. Consider that you have 8 seconds to make an authority figure pay attention to what you have to say, so use your time wisely and use a great hook to make him want to listen.[21]

Prove Your Worth

When coming from a place of low power, you have little going for you beyond your output at work. You must work hard to prove that you are worthy of even gaining your manager's notice and advancing in the workplace or gaining a say. Your boss won't take you too seriously if you are not a dedicated employee who has sound judgement. Being indispensable will increase your value and thus your power.

Being indispensable involves pleasing your manager or boss's needs. Serving him as well as the company will make you a valuable employee. So while you might not see the use in doing personal favors for him, you are really garnishing lots of reciprocity which may pay off in the end.

This hardly means that you should anything and everything for your boss, to the point where you are being taken advantage of. Setting boundaries can define your personality and give you an edge of power in the eyes of your boss. Give him everything you've got – until he asks too much. Then let him know or ask for a day off and state why you feel you deserve it.[22] The idea of setting boundaries stems from neuroscience research and is proven to improve relationships as well as your self-esteem.[22]

Bosses tend to respect and reward those who are indispensable and do good work, yet who demand respect for themselves and are not just doormats.

Setting boundaries will create the difference between the overlooked office brown noser and the budding upper management material on an upward trajectory.

From day one, you should start asserting your dominance and boundaries in the office in subtle ways. Have a confident posture, speak your mind, and demand that people respect your boundaries. Make a big deal about it when someone eats your lunch or calls you a disrespectful name. This behavior only serves to earn you respect and heighten your power. You don't need to break rules or be rude to accomplish this, either.

Also from day one, make yourself indispensable by asking lots of questions. Look up to your boss as a teacher and boost his ego that way. Respect what he says and flatter his importance.[13] Ask what else you can do and find things to do without being told. This all serves him, which appeals to his needs and makes him like you more, leading to the principle of liking coming into play.[8]

Also, prove that you're a go-getter. Intuitively guess what comes next, confirm with your boss to ensure you're not overstepping, and use some autonomy while following directions. Don't be afraid to brainstorm and pitch new ideas or propose meetings. If you come from a place of respect, but volunteer your efforts and your ideas readily, then you can prove yourself as a very valuable part of the company with upper management written on your forehead in capital letters. Giving him choices is also a proven way to appeal to his needs and cement the relationship as a good one.[23] This in turn will help gain the traction necessary to impress him and get him to take you seriously.[8]

Remember Etiquette

Human beings are quite sensitive to etiquette. The last thing you want to do is make a fool of yourself at a party or dinner. Remember etiquette and use good manners at all times to set a good impression.

Always use your table manners. Learn to open doors and pull out chairs for important guests. Standing when someone enters the room is another rule that makes people feel important. These good manners make you look professional and appeal to the egos of your superiors.

Part of etiquette involves your appearance. People respond to the way you look and make snap judgements about you. It would be nice if everyone followed the adage, "Don't judge a book by its cover," but sadly the cover is often the only thing we have to judge by, especially in the business world when people must make many non-personal connections at once.[24]

Therefore, your outward appearance is everything in the business world. You'll never get a second chance – after the first few seconds, people have molded their impression of you and won't bother to reevaluate it in a hurried business interaction.[24] Think about what you want to communicate to others to make them trust you and to make money. Confidence, wealth, resourcefulness, ambition, intelligence, the ability to respect authority while also vying for authority, decisiveness, and dedication are all traits highly valued in the Western business world.

You can communicate these traits in your posture, attire, and approach. A confident posture and body language is the loudest voice in your appearance. The way you carry your body can tell people you have all the above traits. A confident posture entails

Remember that bit about wearing red? That's applicable here too. Or you can wear black to show how serious and confident you are. Blue paints you as an authority figure. Colors really do have an effect on the human brain and will form others' impressions of you.[13]

Asking for Promotions

Asking for a promotion is a nerve-wracking experience. But it is necessary if you want to be considered for a higher salary. Asserting your worth can make your boss notice and appreciate you more. Asking for a promotion or raise calls for a blend of persuasion and appealing to your boss's position of power.

Wait for the Opportunity

Popping the question for a promotion is not ideal when your boss's attention is being held by something else or he is stressed to the max with a current crisis. Microsoft's 2015 study suggests that people in the digital age are far more capable of handling multitasking,[21] but this still doesn't mean that you should bother your boss when he's focused on something else. It is best to wait for a time when there are no crises going on and your boss is in a rather relaxed mood.

Asking directly can earn his respect because you're not beating around the bush, wasting his time and yours. But if your boss seems leery of the idea, it may be better to warm him up to it. Plant the idea of a promotion as a seed in his mind and mention it from time to time so that he becomes conditioned to the idea. He will be more likely to say yes if you condition him slowly over time.

First, ask him if there is a good time to talk. Set up a meeting wherein you discuss your promotion and nothing else. When you have planted the seed, wait for it to germinate and water it frequently by mentioning the promotion whenever the opportunity arises.

Sell Yourself

A great presentation is ideal when you pop the initial question. This presentation allows you to shamelessly sell yourself, using Dr. Cialdini's tried and true principles of influence. Don't downplay your achievements or sought after traits – show them off and use them as evidence that you are the best person for the position you are gunning for.

If you are creating your own position, which is possible in some organizations, then be sure to outline exactly what this position entails. Push how it benefits the company and your boss, by lightening his workload somehow and improving his favor with the higher ups. Mention research you have done and other companies that utilize such a position to gain some authority on the matter.[8]

After you sell your new position, whatever it is, it is time to start selling yourself. Become a used car salesman for yourself, though of course don't be so cheesy.

First, show how valuable you are to the company. Highlight new skills you have learned and weaknesses you have developed during your tenure. Outline exactly how you can use these skills and strengths in your new role. You want to prove authority and value.[8]

Second, show how dedicated you are. Bring up some project you burned midnight oil on, or remind your boss how you always remember his coffee. Mention your loyalty to the company, but also mention that your skill set is in demand to hint at the fact you could go to another company and thus create the scarcity principle in your boss's mind.[8]

Being friendly and warm is a good way to get the liking principle going, as well.[8] Your best bet is to always be this way in the office, to everyone. Being nice only on the day you ask for a promotion is obviously fake and he will be able to tell. On the day you want to ask for a promotion, bring your boss a warm beverage to put warmth in his mind, which will work subliminally in your favor. Use positive, upbeat, can-do language and focus on the future, rather than knocking the work of other people or criticizing the company. If there are problems you plan to solve with your position, mention them in a positive way and focus on the solutions you propose as opposed to the negativity of what is wrong.[2]

If you are going for a position that someone else has vacated, don't be ashamed to point out how you could do better than the previous person. Be sure to stay positive and show the previous person respect by acknowledging his valuable contributions, but add how you can expand on them and how you learned from them to be even better.

Speak in definite terms. You don't want to sound wishy-washy and say things like, "I might be able to do this" or "I really hope you consider this and maybe give me this position!" Instead, show off your confidence by saying, "I am the best person for this job. I look forward to hearing your decision on this matter." Harvard Business Review stresses the importance of using definite terms to impart confidence and a get-it-done attitude.[25]

Finally, always thank your boss for his time. This is just polite etiquette that will ingratiate yourself to him. Remember, manners will always get you far in life.

When all of this is said and done, your boss may have some questions for you. This becomes a lot like the initial job interview that landed you this job. Treat it as such. Harvard Business Review encourages you to put careful thought into each answer – possibly try to preempt questions and consider responses even before entering your boss's office to make your pitch.[25]

Harvard Business Review further pushes using rapport to create a link, or bond, with your boss that makes him like you more.[25] Find things to relate on throughout your presentation and the subsequent interview, such as similar visions for the company or similar pastimes. This makes for a good conversation, impression, and bond.

Summarizing information is encouraged.[25] Summarize what you just said, and then ask if your boss has any questions. This ensures that there are no misunderstandings or oversights.

Relax to instill relaxation and confidence in your boss.[25] Just like negativity is contagious, so is tension.[2] Conveying a positive, relaxed vibe will make you look better and will encourage your boss to receive your presentation more positively. Don't rush to fill the air with words because you can't stand silence, don't babble, and don't fidget.

Dealing with a Bad Boss

When dealing with a bad boss, you are likely to do one of two things: Explode or shrink into yourself and run from the conflict. Neither of these approaches are helpful in getting your way or opening discussion in the workplace. Learning how to actually talk to your boss will be far more conducive to success.

Five Worst Boss Personalities and How to Handle Them

These are five of the worst bosses you may encounter in the workplace:

The narcissists think that the ground they walk on is blessed. Their egos come before work and what is right or best for the company. If they can make you feel bad or inferior, they will. Manipulation and

94

power games are their fortes. Dealing with such a boss involves framing everything in some way that proves how it will serve him or further his goals. You must sell things to him by appealing to his selfish nature.

The passive-aggressive bosses are petty and immature. Your passive-aggressive boss may tell you he loves your work, then tells the rest of the office otherwise. He may belittle you in tiny ways or show that he is irritated with you without explaining why or how you can fix things. He may do things wrong deliberately, just to spite you. Dealing with such a boss entails being very specific in your wording and keeping copies of all communication with him so he can't find some loophole to spite you with.

Gossips are equally manipulative and hurtful. They just do everything behind your back. They can spread lies and really damage your reputation in a company. The first step is to avoid sharing personal information or information that can be twisted and misconstrued. The next step is to confront the gossip to his face. Gossips are sneaky people, so being put on the spot will make them extremely uncomfortable and call their power games into question. It will humiliate them and stop the behavior for a while.

The ignorant boss does everything by the book and hates innovation. They will ignore anything you propose and assume they are right because they are doing everything by precedent. Appealing to an ignorant boss involves really proving why your proposal will work. You may have to keep bothering this boss to capture his attention. Dramatizing your ideas really works here. Another idea is to circumvent your boss and go above his head, which of course won't sit well with him but will get you noticed by higher-ups.

Angry bosses are the ones who love to shout, throw things, and assert their dominance through aggression. They are often scary to work for because you never know when you will trigger rage. To talk to these bosses, try to do it in a public spot where other people can view the interaction. Tape or record angry outbursts to show to HR. Also, be very gentle and try to frame things in a way that will appeal to the boss's ego, to hopefully circumvent his outburst of rage.

Keeping Your Sanity with a Bad Boss

A bad boss can totally sour your workplace and your overall happiness. Separating business and personal is essential to avoid going crazy or becoming depressed when working for a bad boss.

With over 16.1 million Americans depressed, depression is a national health crisis.[26] Many people report feeling stressed or depressed due to their jobs. If you don't want to be a part of this glum statistic, you must take action to avoid letting your job rob you of your happiness.

The main secret to dealing with a bad boss is to find a new job. In the meantime, look on the bright side; since positivity is contagious, it may transfer to your workplace. Consider what experience and skills you are gaining from this job, and possibly a good reference too.

Always compartmentalize. At work, put personal feelings aside. After work, stop thinking about work and enjoy yourself. Have a hobby and don't make the mistake of being married to your job.

How to Gain Ground with Managers who Do Not Respect You

All of the time, you run into dominant managers who don't bother to maintain dialogue with you, or who don't think your opinion matters. A good boss is meant to glean and use the opinions and voices of the whole team, but we all know it's not a perfect world. If you have a manager who doesn't want to hear what you have to say, take action by making yourself heard.

Speak His Language

It can be quite clear if your manager lacks respect for you. According to research by Inc., some of the top reasons that employees feel disrespected include bosses who change their minds constantly, who change what they want the employee to work on, and who micromanage and review everything you do as if they don't trust you. Bosses who don't listen and who need to be chased down for approval also rank high on the list of frustratingly disrespectful behavior.[27]

If your manager doesn't hear or respect you, you need to nab his attention by speaking his language. It is likely that you have opposing interaction styles, which means that communication has faltered and a solid bond has failed to form. Your boss won't bother to change because he is dominant and needs you to come up to his level. Changing your interaction style is a good way to solve this miscommunication.[27]

Contemplators like to be deliberate and take their time. They use facts and data to reach the right decision. To reach such a manager effectively, you should attempt to also use facts and approach him in a clear, deliberate manner. Also take your time when making decisions and do great work. He will start to respect you more.

Commanders just like to give orders. They operate from a place of logic and often don't factor feelings into the equation at all. If they make a mistake, they don't want to hear about it. With such a boss, use action-centered language and use lots of animated hand gestures or presentations to get his attention. Prove to him why what you have to say matters and should factor into the next command he gives. Talking about feelings won't get you anywhere, you want to talk about how you'll take action.

Energizers are full of energy and like to psyche up the office. They don't respect those who are low in spirits or reserved in energy. Using an upbeat tone and a similar enthusiasm is a good way to get him to pay attention to you.

Empathizers are intuitive, emotional, and sensitive. They like to know how everyone is feeling and if the office is up to the task any given day. They tend to speak softly and avoid offending others. Come at this boss with a similar approach and ask him how he feels about certain things. Tell him how you feel, and how the office feels in general. This will mean a lot more to him and will get through to him as opposed to using cold logic and facts.

Similarly, find out how your boss uses sensory perception.[28] Some people are visual and like to read or see pictures. Others are tactile and need to "feel" and interact something in a hands-on way to understand it. Some people like to be told directions. There are even people who favor taste and smell.

You will be able to tell what sense your boss relies on the most heavily by how he talks.[28] If he says, "I see," "I can picture that," or "Picture this" a lot he's a visual kind of guy. If he uses more auditory terms, like "Do you hear me?" or "I hear you," then he's an auditory guy. Finally, if he uses a ton of "feeling" phrases, he's a tactile person.

When you approach him, try to use his sensory language. Match him in asking him if he sees what you're saying, or feels what you're saying. He will relate to you much more efficiently if you use his sensory language. Plus, use his sensory language to figure out how to present information to him. For instance, a PowerPoint would be ideal for a visual person, while a physical hands-on demonstration might work better for a tactile person.

Maximize Interaction

People tend to like you the more they are exposed to you, in what is known as the mere-exposure effect.[29] On the other hand, if you purposefully avoid your manager because you don't care for him or he doesn't care for you, you are making the situation worse. Repeated exposures will get you far more ground over time.

In a study back in the 1960s, a student wore a black bag to class every day for a semester. The other students had no idea who he was. They treated him with hostility at first, but that changed the more they were exposed to him. By the end of the semester, they considered him a friend.[29] This is a fascinating glimpse into how mere exposure works.

So show your face more. Talk more with your manager, forcing interactions if you have to. Always be friendly and polite. Over time, you will notice his respect and favor for you increases. Basically, he will come to like your face and accept you as part of his team.

In rare cases when this fails, you may just need to find a new job. Dealing with a hateful manager can ruin the workplace and increase depression. Don't tolerate it if all of your attempts to fix the issue fail.

Chapter 6: Personal

This final section on conversation skills will teach you the main struggles of dealing with personal communication. What good are conversation skills if you don't know how to employ them in some of life's trickiest situations? Good conversation skills can actually smooth over a lot of icky situations that you may find yourself in and can help you deal with particularly difficult people.

To make your life easier, start to use these professional conversation skills on everyone you know. Even the people you dislike will start to treat you better if you use proper conversation skills on them. You can turn enemies into friends, resolve conflicts, and make people respect you with these tips.

How to Deal with a Disrespectful Person

Dealing with a disrespectful person is never a pleasant experience. Unfortunately, disrespectful people are everywhere. Some of them don't care; others believe that you must work to earn their respect. No matter what, disrespect humiliates you and makes you want to either retreat or fight, neither of which are ever helpful.

Ideally, you can just ignore a disrespectful person. Even though it hurts your feelings, a passing stranger is not worth too much fuss. But that advice becomes impossible to follow when you must deal with this disrespectful regularly. You will run into them at work, at school, in your neighborhood or apartment building, and in any organization you become involved in. Knowing how to shut them down rapidly can make you quake in your shoes, so you may need to take a deep breath, remember that you are worth respect, and then seize that respect by putting this disrespectful person in place.

There is No Need for Aggression

If you show aggression, the other person will too.[31] Aggression is a spiral that quickly gets out of hand. It is fed by stimulus and grows with adrenalin.[31] Therefore, avoid getting mad or showing aggression if you don't want the same response.

Positivity tends to spread.[1] This is why they say, "Kill them with kindness." If you want to have a smooth interaction, don't get angry. Instead, remain positive and calm. Offer a nice smile.[9] A disrespectful person may be so disgruntled that he resists the instinct to smile back, but the smile will throw him off and change the outcome of the situation. It may also make him respect you more in future interactions.

Often times, a person who is disrespectful to you is feeling insecure or angry himself. He feeds off the spread of aggression as an outlet for his own pent-up issues.[31] The result is that he purposefully tries to make you mad. Not giving him what he wants will rapidly diffuse the situation. He will get confused by the unexpected happy response and probably walk away or soften toward you.

Sometimes, people don't even realize they are being disrespectful. They are too busy or distracted to notice how their behavior appears toward others. Some people totally lack empathy and have poor social skills, so they fail to consider how they might be making others feel with their actions. Responding to people in this kind manner will generate better responses because they will learn to like you and will think, "I was being rude just now. I should be nice to this person who is so nice to me." The rule of reciprocity often works here.[8]

Use the Mere Exposure Effect

You learned in the previous chapter to use the mere exposure effect to get rude managers to start to like and respect you. That same principle applies to more personal settings. If a person you know personally is rude to you, frequent exposures will help change his attitude from hostile to friendly.[29]

Just as the student in the black bag proved, the more this person sees you, the friendlier he should become. Don't go hide away or avoid interactions with this person. Instead, stick your neck and purposefully put yourself in the way of interaction. In time, he will probably start to like you enough to show you respect.

Anyone who has been terrorized by a bully for years knows that mere exposure is not always 100% effective. Some people have it out for you from day one and their dislike and disrespect only worsens with time. If repeated exposures don't seem to help, then it may be time to set some boundaries and assert some dominance.

Prove Dominance

The best way to win the respect of others is to prove your own dominance.[19] Only when you're top dog will other people treat you as such. Often, people make snap judgements about others, so the way you present yourself can determine if they want to respect you or not.[24]

The first step is to use a more firm, deep voice and a more dominant posture.[19] Don't be afraid to look this disrespectful person directly in the eye and be the last to look away.[19] These are instinctually understood dominance signals. Performing these moves will prove that you will no longer accept subpar treatment and that you are starting to demand better. Many disrespectful people who are used to walking all over will become surprised by this sudden display of dominance, and will usually retreat and start to show a different attitude to you.

Others will take this new display of dominance as a challenge and will rear their heads in an attempt to put you back in your place, at least the place they think you should occupy. They take part in the eternal dominance struggle that humans undergo for their entire lives.[19]

Just hold your ground, don't break eye contact, and keep a smile on your face. Pretend their aggression does not scare or bother you. When they realize they can't win with you or provoke you, they will give up and back down. And you just earned yourself a decent helping of respect.

The dominance struggle is fluid and ever-changing.[19] The dominant person today can become the submissive one tomorrow. If you have been disrespected, start the struggle and make sure you emerge on top by never backing down. You will gain far more respect this way and you will deal with less disrespect in the future as a result.

Set Healthy Boundaries

The best thing to do when a person is disrespectful to you is to set boundaries. Many humans don't bother to do this out of fear of provoking the other person's anger. But typically, a disrespectful person will begin to thaw and respect you more when you prove that you won't tolerate their treatment. Starting today, lay out the rules.

It is very simple, though nerve-wracking, to look at a disrespectful person and say, "You may not speak to me that way." That sets a huge boundary and proves your dominance. Plus, it gives you the element of surprise, because this person is not used to others standing up to him.

When a person interrupts you, say, "Hold on, I wasn't finished talking" and then calmly and boldly continue. This will also shock many people who are used to power talking through everyone else. It gives you a very dominant demeanor that most people are going to respect.

Call out other unacceptable behavior in the same manner. If a person tends to swing doors shut in your face, for instance, speak up and say that is unacceptable. Declare that you are a human being and you are entering the building as well so you don't need someone slamming doors in your face.

Confrontation that is direct and clear is the best way to handle such bullies. Speak up about the boundary you want to set in front of others and be very clear and adamant. Doing this in front of other people will enable you to feel stronger and will minimize the negative response you get in return. Out of humiliation, the bull will probably not do anything in response, and if he does, then he looks bad in front of everyone and that is even more humiliating. Humiliation is never a good tactic, but if you are dealing with a bully, a public call-out is often more beneficial than a private chat.

Through social proof, you can get more people on your side and possibly gain more traction with the disrespectful person in question.[8] While this works on occasion, people tend to be afraid of bullies, so you may be on your own with this one. Nevertheless, stand your ground and others may catch onto the trend, allowing the disrespectful person to lose his position of power.[8]

Be sure to use commitment and consistency, especially with a disrespectful person who continues to push you.[8] Every time this person violates a boundary, speak up. Don't speak up once and then let it slide every time after, or you will lose some of your respect in the bully's eyes. Consistent boundary setting will ultimately win the day.

How to Handle a Conversation Where You Are Right and the Other Person is Obviously Not

Almost all verbal disagreements stem from people treating opinions as fact and swearing up and down they are right. This tendency to have to be right is because of a psychological phenomena known as "the confirmation bias."[30] A person will develop some opinion and then twist and bend every bit of information he receives to prove himself right. This is why you can't win an argument with most people.

When you enter a conversation where you happen to know you're right, nothing is more infuriating than going up against a person who is utterly wrong. This person will refuse to accept he's wrong and will argue with you till he's blue in the face, defending his position at the risk of looking like an idiot. His confirmation bias will enable him to keep proving himself right...even though he clearly isn't!

Pick Your Battles

Life is pretty stressful, and fighting spikes your stress levels even more. In fact, fighting with another person, even if the fighting isn't violent, creates an adrenalin spike for a fight or flight response. Your heart rate gets elevated, your blood sounds pounding, and you get angrier as your adrenalin leads to a rush.[31] Anger may quickly spiral completely out of control and even turn violent if you keep letting the stress build up within you.[31]

Therefore, it is never healthy to fight with someone. Minimizing stress is beneficial for your health, and can prevent heart diseases and improve your immune system.[32] The last thing you want to do is kill yourself over fights that don't matter.

This is why you should pick your battles. It isn't just an old saying, it's true scientific wisdom as well. Is this fight really worth it? Do you really need to be right? Chances are fair that, no, you don't need to win this or be right. So just let it go. There's no point wasting energy and adrenalin on a stubborn person who will probably one day find out he's wrong on his own anyway.

However, there are instances when you absolutely must be right. Work in a scientific lab, in a pharmacy, or with weapons are just a few of many examples where precision means the difference between life or death. If someone is wrong and about to make a huge mistake, you might just have to enter battle and endure some stress for the good of mankind. Fighting about your children or other important things in your life also matters.

Before fighting with someone on whether he's right or wrong, evaluate how life or death this matter is. Proceed only if you think it truly matters. Being right for the good of your own ego is not a legitimate reason to put yourself through so much stress.

Acknowledge He Thinks He's Right

Giving someone some validation of his emotions makes him feel important and heard.[13] That's usually all people want from any interaction. Before proving your point and why you are right, start by acknowledging, "I can see why you think this." Say that even if you have no idea how this person could be so wrong!

Repeating what he says back to him can ensure that there is no miscommunication going on. Sometimes a person may seem wrong but really he's saying something right and you are misunderstanding it. You would be surprised how often this happens. Clear up what is being said before you move on to proving him wrong.

Next, assure him that you agree with some points of what he is saying, but you have credible evidence to support a different fact. Now this is your chance to move onto the next step and actually prove him wrong. Most people don't like to admit they are wrong, but if you have solid proof, you can make it impossible for them to argue and refute the evidence any longer.

Whip Out Some Cold Hard Facts

Thanks to confirmation bias, sometimes even facts don't stand ground with an obstinate person who is determined to be right. He will somehow refute the credibility of said facts, or he will filter the information to somehow suit his agenda. The end result is that facts are not always the best way to win a fight with such a person.

However, it can be hard to argue with credible facts. A person who does is often just an idiot and everyone else will be able to tell that. Go to reputable sources to find your facts. Wikipedia is not a reputable source; look for peer-reviewed papers or educational sites for your information. Visit famous and important books written by scholars. Draw on expert opinions and advice.

Cold, hard facts are hard to argue with. A person will usually realize what he's up against and thus back down. But if a person won't, well, you are dealing with a true hardhead. You will never win. At least others can tell you are right and he is wrong and you can get more support that way.

Based on social proof, if more people support you than the other party, then you have a winning argument and a better chance of getting the other party to admit he's wrong.[8] Use cold, hard facts to get people on your side. The more popular your statement becomes, the harder it will be for him to argue with.

Call on an Expert

Authority is another influence principle that works wonders when it comes to arguing with a person.[8] If you can find an expert in something to give his opinion in support of your argument, then you can convince the other person you are right more easily. You can call on an expert you know or find one online who says exactly what you are saying.

Most people assume they are right, but they back down when they see an authority figure.[8] They assume, sometimes incorrectly, that an authority figure is more apt to be correct and they give that person more respect. So while a person who is wrong may not respect what you have to say, he will be more likely to admit he's wrong when faced with an authority figure's opinion.

If you can't find an expert, try to get another authority figure on your side. The kind of authority figure depends upon the situation. If you are dealing with a legal issue, find a lawyer or get the cops involves to prove that you are on the right side of the law. If you are involved in a conflict at work, see if you can get your boss or a senior employee to settle the dispute. Hopefully the authority figure sides with you because that's your ticket to proving your correctness totally.

Use Ethos, Pathos, and Logos to Your Advantage

Conversing with a person who is in the wrong involves a level of persuasion. The science of persuasive speaking and writing typically calls on the use of these three things because they work on three things the human brain likes: emotional empathy, logic, and ethics.

Talk about the ethos, or ethics, of something to convince a person that what he is doing is wrong. Any ethical person will rethink his actions and feel a degree of guilt at this point.

Use pathos and discuss emotions. Ask him how others might feel if he persists on being wrong. Ask him how he might feel when he's proved wrong in front of lots of people. Find some emotional component to the argument and use that.

Use logos and appeal to his logical side with the cold, hard facts. Talk about how what you're saying makes the most sense. Presenting a clear, factual argument is hard to refute.

Don't Actively Humiliate Him

In every situation, you have two choices: Be nasty about it or be nice about it. Always select the latter option. Not doing so can breed resentment that will haunt your relationship forever.

Remember, humiliation is an extremely powerful emotion.[17] It is akin to having a leg broken or being rejected. You don't want to inflict this feeling on a person, or you will probably be the object of his hatred for years to come. While it can be satisfying to humiliate someone, it is not a wise plan.

Avoid proving him wrong in front of a lot of people, particularly people he may be trying to impress. A boss, a girlfriend or boyfriend, a potential date, his children – these are people whose opinions he really values. Also don't gloat and flaunt how you were right or rub his face in the matter. Drop it and don't bring it up again once he admits he was wrong. This will prevent an arch nemesis from forming.

Conclusion

Conversation skills have eluded you thus far in life. But now you realize that they are not so elusive or complicated after all. They are just skills that you can learn on your own.

Conversation is the face of human interaction. Lots of science, including psychology, sociology, and chemistry, goes on behind the scenes. Understanding this science makes conversation accessible to even the most awkward person.

Being able to relate to other human beings is essential for your health and happiness in life. Conversation enables you to make new connections, bond with other people, and find new opportunities. You make good impressions on others and thus get ahead in life. It is essential to have good conversation skills.

If you suffer from poor conversation skills, life has been tougher than it needs to be thus far. But now all that is about to change. Using the solid and science-backed tips covered in these pages, you are set to find a new way in life.

Always refer back to this book if you need to. Just bear in mind that having good conversation is really quite simple. Stay on point, evoke emotion in the other person, get personal quickly, and always try to find similarities. These tips are foolproof ways to connect with others more effectively.

Conversation skills get trickier when you introduce such things as persuasion or changing another person. But even these subjects are more than possible to tackle with science. There are certain proven hacks to persuading and changing other people without causing offence. These are covered in Chapters 3 and 4 and will change your life.

Imagine the power you have to change the lives of others and improve your own life if you are able to persuade, convince, and change others. These are skills possessed by strong leaders and powerful speakers, and they can be your skills with some practice.

Business and personal conversations are vastly different. This is why they need to be approached and treated differently. Business conversations need to be warm, inviting, and convincing, while personal ones need to be emotional, sincere, and friendly. Understanding these differences can prevent you from getting too friendly with your boss – or too cold with your significant other.

Like all skills, conversation takes some practice. Practice on good friends or strangers such as baristas and bartenders. The more you practice conversation, the more neural pathways your brain builds. Soon, conversation becomes effortless because your brain knows exactly how to do it. You will not struggle with conversation, or making friends and persuading people, much longer.

You will enjoy the success that comes with good conversation skills. Your life will improve in all areas that are impacted by social interaction. Don't put it off any longer. Start learning and practicing good conversation skills today and notice the impact it has on your day-to-day existence.

References

1.Stillman, et al. *Valence asymmetries in the human amygdala: task relevance modulates amygdala responses to positive more than negative affective cues.* Journal of Cognitive Neuroscience. 2015 Apr;27(4):842-51. doi: 10.1162/jocn_a_00756. Epub 2014, Nov 12.

2. Rohini Ahluwalia, Robert E. Burnkrant, H. Rao Unnava (*2000*) *Consumer Response to Negative Publicity: The Moderating Role of Commitment.* Journal of Marketing Research: May 2000, Vol. 37, No. 2, pp. 203-214.

3. Raymundo Báez-Mendoza* and Wolfram Schultz. *The role of the striatum in social behavior.* Frontier Neuroscience. 2013; 7: 233. Published online 2013 Dec 10. Prepublished online 2013 Nov 5. doi: [10.3389/fnins.2013.00233]

4. Changing Minds. Different Types of Listening.
http://changingminds.org/techniques/listening/types_listening.htm.

5. Hibbs, Dave (2011). Effects of Emotional Intensity and Type of Appeal on Motivation. *The Huron University College Journal of Learning and Motivation*: Vol. 49 : Iss. 1 , Article 3.
Available at: https://ir.lib.uwo.ca/hucjlm/vol49/iss1/3

6. Bahns, AJ. (2016). *Similarity in Relationships as Niche Construction: Choice, Stability, and Influence within Dyads.* Journal of Personality and Social Psychology, 11(2): pp. 329-355. DOI: 10.1037/pspp0000088.

7. Aron, Arthur, et al. (1997). *The Experimental Generation of Personal Closeness: A Procedure and Some Preliminary Findings.* PSPB, Vol 23, No. 4, pp. 363-377.
https://journals.sagepub.com/doi/pdf/10.1177/01461 67297234003.

8. Cialdini, R. (2006). *Influence: The Psychology of Persuasion.* Harper Business. ISBN-13: 978-0061241895.

9. O'Doherty, J., et al. (2003). *Beauty in a Smile: The Role of the Medial Orbitofrontal Cortex in Facial Attractiveness.* Neuropsychologia. 2003;41(2):147-55.

10.Wiseman, et al. (2015). *The Eyes Don't Have It: Lie Detection and Neuro-Linguistic Programming.* PLoS ONE. 7, 7, 5 p. e40259

11.Carmody, D. & Lewis, M. (2006). *Brain Activation When Hearing One's Own And Others' Names.* Brain Res. 2006 Oct 20; 1116(1): 153–158. DOI: 10.1016/j.brainres.2006.07.121

12.Maslow, Abraham. (1943). *A Theory of Human Motivation.* Psychological Review.

13. Elliot, et al. (2010). *Red, Rank, and Romance in Women Viewing Men.* American Psychology Association, 0096-3445/10/. DOI: 10.1037/a0019689

14.Riess, H. (2017). *The Science of Empathy.* J Patient Exp. 2017 Jun; 4(2): 74–77. Published online 2017 May 9. doi: 10.1177/2374373517699267

15.Carnegie, Dale. (2009 reissue). *How to Win Friends and Influence People.* Simon & Schuster. ISBN-13: 978-1439167342.

16. Baumeister, R. (2001). *Bad Is Stronger than Good.* Review of General Psychology, 5(4), 323-370. http://dx.doi.org/10.1037/1089-2680.5.4.323

17. Otten, M. & Jonas, KJ. (2014). *Humiliation as an Intense Emotional Experience: Evidence from the Electro-Encephalogram.* Social Neuroscience, 9(1):23-35. doi: 10.1080/17470919.2013.855660.

18.Nevin, J. & Mandell, C. (2017). *Comparing Positive and Negative Reinforcement: A Fantasy Experiment.* J Exp Anal Behav., 107(1):34-38. doi: 10.1002/jeab.237.

19. Ligneul, R., et al. (2016). *Dynamical Representations of Dominance Relationships in the Human Rostromedial Prefrontal Cortex.* PubMed, 5;26(23):3107-3115. doi: 10.1016/j.cub.2016.09.015.

20.Anderson, R. & Klofstad, C. (2012). *Preference for leaders with Masculine Voices Holds in the Case of Feminine Leadership Roles.* Plos One. • https://doi.org/10.1371/journal.pone.0051216.

21.Microsoft. (2015). *People Have Shorter Attention Spans than Goldfish.* https://www.scribd.com/document/265348695/Microsoft-Attention-Spans-Research-Report.

22. Positive Psychology Program. (2018). *How to Set Healthy Boundaries.* https://positivepsychologyprogram.com/great-self-care-setting-healthy-boundaries/.

23.Ybarra, O., et al. (2012). *Supportive Social Relationships Attenuate the Appeal of Choice.* Psychological Science. Vol 23, Issue 10, https://doi.org/10.1177/0956797612440458

24. Willis, J. & Todorov, A. (2006). *First Impressions: Making Up Your Mind After a 100-Ms Exposure to a Face.* Psychological Science. Vol. 17, Issue 7, https://doi.org/10.1111/j.1467-9280.2006.01750.x.

25. Trull, Samuel. (1964). *Strategies of Effective Interviewing.* Harvard Business Review. https://hbr.org/1964/01/strategies-of-effective-interviewing.

26. Anxiety & Depression Association of America. (2018). *Facts and Statistics.* https://adaa.org/about-adaa/press-room/facts-statistics.

27. O'Donnell. (2018). *7 Warning Signs Your Boss Disrespects You.* WorkItDaily. https://www.inc.com/jt-odonnell/7-warning-signs-your-boss-disrespects-you.html.

28. Bandler, Richard. (2013). *The Ultimate Guide to NLP.* Harper Collins. ISBN-13: 978-0007497416.

29. Zajonc, R. (1968). *Attitudinal Effects of Mere Exposure.* University of Michigan. Journal of Psychology and Social Psychology Monogram Supplment, Vol. 9, No. 2, Part 2. http://web.mit.edu/curhan/www/docs/Articles/biases/9_J_Personality_Social_Psychology_1_%28Zajonc%29.pdf.

30. Nickerson, R. (1998). *Confirmation Bias: An Uniquitous Phenomenon in Many Guises.* Tufts University. Review of General Psychology, Vol. 2, No. 2, pp. 175-220. https://pdfs.semanticscholar.org/70c9/3e5e38a8176590f69c0491fd63ab2a9e67c4.pdf

31. Averill, J. (1983). *Anger and Aggression.* University of Massachusetts. American Psychologist. Pp. 1145- 1160.

http://citeseerx.ist.psu.edu/viewdoc/download?doi=1
0.1.1.473.6194&rep=rep1&type=pdf.

32. WebMD. (2018). *Stress Symptoms.*
https://www.webmd.com/balance/stress-
management/stress-symptoms-effects of-stress-on-
the-body#1.

Disclaimer

The information contained in **"Conversation Skills Secrets"** and its components, is meant to serve as a comprehensive collection of strategies that the author of this eBook has done research about. Summaries, strategies, tips and tricks are only recommendations by the author, and reading this eBook will not guarantee that one's results will exactly mirror the author's results.

The author of this Ebook has made all reasonable efforts to provide current and accurate information for the readers of this eBook. The author and its associates will not be held liable for any unintentional errors or omissions that may be found.

The material in the Ebook may include information by third parties. Third party materials comprise of opinions expressed by their owners. As such, the author of this eBook does not assume responsibility or liability for any third party material or opinions.

The publication of third party material does not constitute the author's guarantee of any information, products, services, or opinions contained within third party material. Use of third party material does not guarantee that your results will mirror our results. Publication of such third party material is simply a recommendation and expression of the author's own opinion of that material.

Whether because of the progression of the Internet, or the unforeseen changes in company policy and editorial submission guidelines, what is stated as fact at the time of this writing may become outdated or inapplicable later.

whole or in parts. No parts of this report may be reproduced or retransmitted in any forms whatsoever without the written expressed and signed permission from the author.

Made in the USA
Lexington, KY
22 July 2019